TERMINOLOGY EXTRACTION FOR TRANSLATION AND INTERPRETATION MADE EASY

How to use ChatGPT and other low-cost, web-based programs to create terminology extraction lists and glossaries quickly and easily

Uwe Muegge

ISBN Paperback: 979-8-9893043-1-8

ISBN Hardcover: 979-8-9893043-2-5

Table of Contents

A few tips for using this book

The following guidelines will help you better understand the book's content.

Terminology	If you see a term that you don't know: the definitions in the glossary explain how I use certain terms in this book.
Italics	This font means that this is a reference to another step.
Bold	This font means that this is an element of a program's user interface.
`Typewriter`	This font means that this is text you enter.
→	This symbol means that this is the result when you complete a step correctly.
🗣	This symbol means that this is information that helps you complete a step correctly.

A (very) short introduction to terminology extraction

What's terminology extraction?

A few definitions

- Terminology: the important words in a field of knowledge.
- Terminology extraction: the process of collecting terms.
- Terminology extraction list: a document that contains a collection of terms.
- Glossary: a document that contains the terms and their definitions that are used in a project or a field of knowledge.

A few methods for terminology extraction

Manual method

- You review the full source document to collect terminology.
- You manually create lists that are as complete as needed.

- Works with any language, is very accurate, but can be very time-consuming.

Frequency-based method

- Creates lists based on how often a word appears in a text.
- Creates lists that may miss many terms and may include many words that are not terms.
- Works with many languages, can be very accurate with manual revision, but can be time-consuming.

Wordlist Tool uses the frequency-based method.

Linguistic method

- Creates lists based on an understanding of the structure of a language.
- Creates lists that may miss a few terms and may include a few words that are not terms.
- Works only with a few languages, can be accurate without manual revision, and can be very efficient.

Sketch Engine / OneClick Terms uses the linguistic method.

Large language model method

- Creates lists based on a language model that was built from large amounts of text.
- Creates lists that may miss very few terms and may include very few words that are not terms.

- Works with many languages, can be very accurate without manual revision, can be extremely efficient.

ChatGPT uses the large language model method.

What are the benefits of terminology extraction?

Better understanding of the difficulty of a translation project

- The word count of a source document alone is not always the best basis for planning a translation project.
- You can use the word count together with a terminology extraction list to create more accurate estimates and project plans.

Fewer interruptions during translation

- When you have a terminology extraction list, you can create a project-specific glossary before you begin to translate.
- When you translate with a project-specific glossary, you don't have to interrupt translating to do term research.

Shorter delivery time

- When you translate with a project-specific glossary, you may be able to complete your translation project sooner.
- Once translation is complete, you can use your project-specific glossary with an automatic terminology checker. When you use an automatic terminology checker, you may be able to complete the quality assurance process sooner.

Improved quality

- Using a project-specific glossary ensures terminological consistency, which is an important part of the quality of a translation project.
- If you use machine translation, a project-specific glossary can improve terminological consistency and the accuracy of translated terms.

Happier clients

- Clients who care about quality will be happy that you create a project-specific glossary to ensure terminological consistency.
- Any client will be happy that you may be able to offer shorter delivery times when you create a project-specific glossary.

Easier differentiation from competitors

- Not all language specialists extract terminology and create project-specific glossaries.
- You may have an advantage when you mention to possible new clients that you create project-specific dictionaries.

More joy of work

- When you extract terminology, create project-specific glossaries, and translate without interruptions, you may enjoy your work more.

What's special about the terminology extraction programs described in this book?

More languages

- Traditional terminology extraction programs that produce high-quality results work only with a few languages.
- All of the programs described in this book can extract terminology from dozens of languages.

Lower cost

- ChatGPT and Wordlist Tool are available for free.
- OneClick Terms in anonymous mode with limited functionality is available for free. The full version of OneClick Terms is available for a low monthly subscription.

Easier to use

- OneClick Terms and Wordlist Tool have an intuitive interface. You can extract terminology with both of these programs with a few simple clicks.
- ChatGPT has one of the simplest user interfaces possible. You operate the program by entering simple prompts.

More information

- ChatGPT can add data in additional data categories to terminology extraction lists, including definitions and translated terms.
- **Important**: ChatGPT can provide misleading or incorrect information. You can use ChatGPT to translate terms or to define terms. But for unfamiliar terms or when ChatGPT misinterprets the context, ChatGPT may provide incorrect definitions or translated terms. That means that using ChatGPT to define or translate unknown terms is not a substitute for doing term research.

No installation

- All of these programs are web-based. Web-based programs process data on a server that you can access on the internet through a web browser.

- If you have a web browser installed, you don't need to install any new programs on your computer. Also, web-based programs are automatically updated, which means that you always have access to the latest version.

More operating systems

- All of these programs run on all popular operating systems, including Apple macOS, Apple OS, Google Android, Linux, and Microsoft Windows.

- That means that with a web browser and an internet connection, you can use these programs on any computer.

Higher speed

- All of these programs are web-based. Web-based programs process data on a server that you can access on the internet through a web browser.

- That means that with a fast internet connection, you can create terminology extraction lists almost instantly, even on older computers.

Which of these terminology extraction programs is best for you?

ChatGPT

ChatGPT is a chatbot, a web-based program from OpenAI. This is the program that will most likely produce the best results for most language specialists.

Benefits

- Works with more languages than traditional terminology extraction programs that produce high-quality results.
- Can reliably extract single-part terms, long multi-part terms, and complex expressions.
- Can automatically add data categories to each term: part of speech, gender, number, and many others.
- Can add definitions to each term, which is something none of the traditional terminology extraction programs can do.
- Can add translated terms in one or more of the languages the program works with to each term.
- Is available for free.
- Is very flexible and easy to customize.

Drawbacks

- Has limits on text size as well as the number of requests.
- Saves and potentially shares uploaded text (opt-out available).
- Doesn't have a user interface for terminology extraction, which means you may have to experiment more compared to specialized programs.
- Requires manual copying and pasting of text.
- Can't provide reliable numbers for word frequency.
- Can provide misleading or incorrect information. You can use ChatGPT to translate terms or to define terms. But for unfamiliar terms or when ChatGPT misinterprets the context, ChatGPT may provide incorrect definitions or translated terms. That means that using ChatGPT to define or translate unknown terms is not a substitute for doing term research.
- Is not available in some countries.

A paid version of ChatGPT (ChatGPT Pro) is available for a monthly subscription fee of USD 20. ChatGPT Pro has the same limitations on text size as the free version. ChatGPT Pro may be a good option in the following situations:

- You need more frequent access to ChatGPT than the free version allows.
- You need higher availability of ChatGPT than the free version allows.

Alternative 1: OneClick Terms

OneClick Terms is a web-based program that's based on the text analysis program Sketch Engine from Lexical Computing. If you are willing to pay for a subscription, OneClick Terms can solve some of ChatGPT's limitations.

Benefits

- Doesn't have limits on text size or the number of requests.
- Works with many of the major world languages.
- Can extract single-part terms, multi-part terms, and expressions.
- Can automatically add data categories to each term: part of speech, example sentence.
- Has a simple user interface for controlling the terminology extraction process.
- Can provide reliable numbers for word frequency.
- Is available in countries where ChatGPT isn't available.

Drawbacks

- Requires a paid monthly subscriptions of about USD 15 – 20 per month, depending on your location (you can try out OneClick Terms in anonymous mode for free).
- Works only with the following languages:

Afrikaans	Korean
Chinese Simplified	Māori
Chinese Traditional	Norwegian
Croatian	Norwegian Bokmål
Czech	Norwegian Nynorsk
Danish	Polish
Dutch	Portuguese
English ★	Russian
Estonian ★	Serbian
Finnish	Serbian (Latin)
French ★	Slovak
German ★	Slovenian
Hungarian	Spanish ★
Italian ★	Swedish
Japanese	

- Can extract multi-part terms and expressions for only seven languages (marked with ★ in the list of languages the program works with).

- Can't add definitions to terms.

- Can't add translated terms to terms.

- Has difficulty extracting complex multi-part terms and longer expressions in all languages the program works with.

- Is not as flexible as ChatGPT nor as easy to customize as ChatGPT.

Alternative 2: Wordlist Tool

Wordlist Tool is a web-based program for creating wordlists that was developed by Birmingham City University. If you are willing to do more of the work yourself, Wordlist Tool can solve some of ChatGPT's limitations.

Benefits

- Doesn't have limits on text size or the number of requests.
- Is designed for English but can be used for other languages that separate words with a space.
- Is an efficient program for manually creating the most complete terminology extraction lists.
- Has an extremely simple user interface.
- Can provide reliable numbers for word frequency.
- Is available in countries where ChatGPT isn't available.
- Is available for free.

Drawbacks

- Is not an automatic terminology extraction program but creates lists of all words that appear in a source document.
- Can't extract multi-part terms and expressions.
- Can't add definitions to terms.

- Can't add translated terms to terms.
- Requires more time and effort for creating a terminology extraction list than the other programs.
- Doesn't work with languages that do not separate words with a space (examples: Chinese, Japanese, and Korean).
- Is not as flexible as ChatGPT nor as easy to customize as ChatGPT.

Comparison table

	CHATGPT	ONECLICK TERMS	WORDLIST TOOL
COST	Available for free	About USD 15 -20 per month (depending on your location)	Available for free
LANGUAGES THE PROGRAM WORKS WITH	100+ (estimated)	29	English and other languages that separate words with a space
LIMIT ON TEXT SIZE	16 000 characters (estimated)	No limit	No limit
NUMBER OF REQUESTS	Can be very limited during peak times	No limit	No limit

AUTOMATIC EXTRACTION OF TERMS	Yes	Yes	No (only lists all words that appear in a source text)
AUTOMATIC EXTRACTION OF MULTI-PART TERMS, EXPRESSIONS	Yes	Yes, but only for seven languages	No
AUTOMATIC EXTRACTION OF ADDITIONAL LINGUISTIC DATA CATEGORIES	Yes, many can be customized (Examples: Part of Speech, Example Sentence, Definition, Translated Term)	Yes, limited to two (Part of Speech, Example Sentence)	Yes, limited to 1 (Example Sentence)
AUTOMATIC CALCULATION OF RELIABLE WORD FREQUENCY DATA	No	Yes	Yes
PRIVACY OF THE DATA YOU UPLOAD	By default, ChatGPT shares the data that you upload, but you can opt out of data sharing	OneClick Terms doesn't share the data that you upload	Wordlist Tool doesn't share the data that you upload

Bard AI and Bing Chat

Currently, I don't recommend Bard AI and Bing Chat as suitable alternatives to ChatGPT for terminology extraction. Both chatbots have serious drawbacks compared to ChatGPT.

Bard AI drawbacks

- Has a much smaller limit on text size than ChatGPT. That means that extracting terminology from long source texts can take much longer in Bard AI than in ChatGPT.
- Works with fewer languages than ChatGPT.

Bing Chat drawbacks

- Doesn't allow you to opt out of data sharing. That means that it is not safe to extract terminology from source texts that are confidential.
- Has a smaller limit on text size than ChatGPT. That means that extracting terminology from long source texts can take much longer in Bing Chat than in ChatGPT.
- Has a limit on the number of turns per chat as well as the number of chats per day.

How to use ChatGPT to extract terminology

Creating an account

Enter your email

1. In your web browser, in the address bar: enter the following web address:
   https://chat.openai.com/auth/login

   → The web page **Welcome to ChatGPT** opens.

2. Click the button **Sign up.**

   → The web page **Create your account** opens.

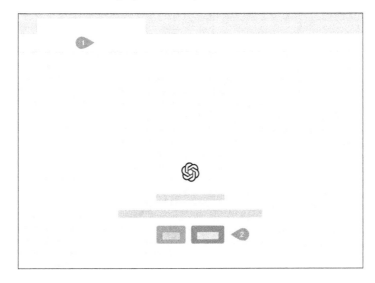

3. On the web page **Create your account,** in the field **Email address:** enter your email address.

   🗣 It's important that you enter your correct email address in this field. OpenAI sends an activation code to the email address you enter in this field.

4. In the field **I'm not a robot:** click the check box.

   🗣 You may have to complete a captcha in this step.

5. Click the button **Continue**.

   → The web page **Create your account opens.**

6. On the web page **Create your account,** in the field
   Password: enter a password that is difficult for
   others to guess.

   🗣 Your password must be at least eight characters
   long. Include numbers and special characters
   in your password. It is best to create different
   passwords for different accounts.

7. Click the button **Continue**.

   → The web page **Verify your mail box** opens.

Look for an email from OpenAI in your email system

1. In your email system: open the folder **Inbox**.

2. Look for an email from <u>noreply@tm.openai.com</u>

🗣 If you can't find that email in your email system: look for that email in your junk folder.

3. Open the email from OpenAI.

4. In the email: click the link **Verify email address.**

→ The web page **Tell us about you** opens.

Enter your Name

1. On the web page **Tell us about you**, in the field **First Name**: enter your first name.

2. In the field **Last Name**: enter your last name.

3. To read the terms of use: click the link **Terms**.

🗣 This step is optional. Use this option to get information about possible risks when you use ChatGPT.

4. Click the button **Continue**.

→ The web page **Verify your phone number** opens.

5. When you click the button **Continue**, you confirm that you are at least 18 years old, and that you agree to the terms of use for ChatGPT.

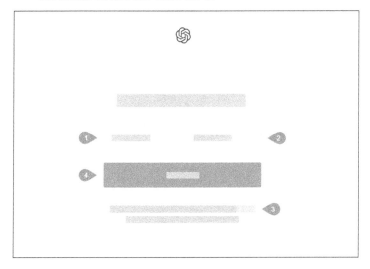

Enter your phone number

1. On the web page **Verify your phone number**: click the button **Country**.

   → A new menu opens.

2. In the new menu: find the name of the country in which your phone is registered, and then click the name of that country.

   → The phone country code for the country that you selected appears in the field **Phone number.**

3. In the field **Phone number:** enter your **phone number**.

🗣 It's important that you enter the phone number of a smartphone that can receive text messages. OpenAI sends an activation code to the phone number that you enter in that field.

4. Click the button **Send code.**

→ The web page **Enter code** opens.

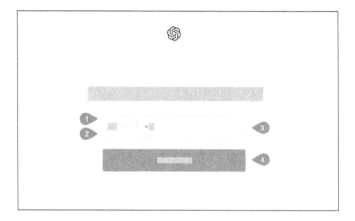

Enter the OpenAI verification code

1. On your smartphone: open your messages app.

2. Open the text message from OpenAI. The verification code is the number that appears after the colon (:).

3. On your computer, on the web page **Enter code:** enter the verification code from the text message.

➔ The web page **ChatGPT** opens.

🗩 If you can't find the text message with the verification code in the messages app on your smartphone: click the link **Resend the code** on the web page **Enter code.**

Navigate to the ChatGPT website

1. In your web browser, in the address bar: enter the following web address:
   https://chat.openai.com/auth/login

   ➔ The web page **Welcome to ChatGPT** opens.

2. Click the button **Log in**.

→ The web page **Welcome back** opens.

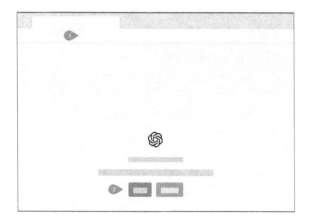

3. On the web page **Welcome back**, in the field **Email address:** enter your email address.

4. Click the button **Continue**.

→ The web page **Enter your password** opens.

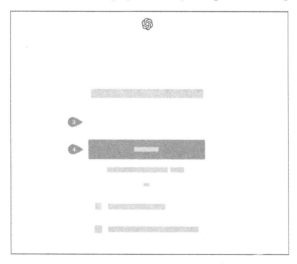

5. On the web page **Enter your password,** in the field **Password**: enter your password.

   🗣 You created your password in *Step 6* of the task *Sign up for an account in ChatGPT.*

6. Click the button **Continue**.

   → The web page **ChatGPT** opens.

Opt out of data collection

🗣 This task is optional. Use this option if you don't want Open AI to collect the data that you enter into ChatGPT and possibly share that data with others. When you enter your client's data in ChatGPT, it is best to use this option to keep that data confidential.

1. On the web page ChatGPT: click **your email.**

   → A new menu opens.

2. In the new menu: click the button **Settings**.

   → The window **Settings** opens.

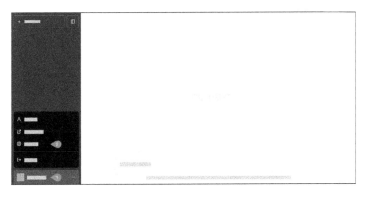

3. In the window **Settings**: click the button **Data controls.**

   → The data control options are displayed.

4. Click the toggle **Chat history & training.**

   → The toggle switches off the function **Chat history & training.**

   🗣 When you opt out of data sharing, Open AI will not share your data with others. But Open AI will also delete all chats that are older than 30 days.

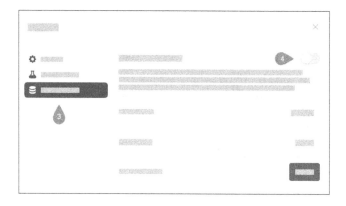

Finding terms

Create a simple terminology extraction list with ChatGPT

🗣 Creating a simple terminology extraction list, in combination with the word count, can help you create more accurate estimates. For projects that require term research, simple terminology extraction lists are not ideal. For those kinds of projects, it's better to create either a monolingual glossary or a multilingual glossary.

1. Open your source document in a suitable program. Select and copy the text from which you want to extract terms.

2. On the web page **ChatGPT**, in the field **Send a message:** enter one of the following prompts:

   🗣 Click the button **Clear chat** near the top of the web page before you enter a prompt. This step clears the chat history, which means that your prompt is not influenced by previous conversations. If you have chat history enabled: Click the button **New chat**.

```
Create a numbered list of the
terminology that is used in the
following text.
```

🗣 Creating a numbered list is optional. Use this option if you are looking for an easy way to count the number of terms in a terminology extraction list.

```
Create a list of the important terms
that are used in the following text.
```

```
Create a list of the words and
expressions in the following text that
may be difficult to translate.
```

🗣 Try out different variations of these prompts to get the best result.

3. After the prompt that you just entered: paste the text that you copied in *Step 1* into the field **Send a message.**

4. Click the **arrow symbol** > in the field **Send a message.**

🗣 ChatGPT creates a terminology extraction list for the text that you entered.

5. Once ChatGPT has created a terminology extraction list: click the button **Regenerate**.

→ ChatGPT creates another terminology extraction list for the text that you entered.

🗣 *Steps 5-7* are optional. Use this option to create multiple terminology extraction lists and then select the one that fits your project best.

6. Once you have created several versions of the terminology extraction list: click the < > arrows at the top of the terminology extraction list to navigate between the different versions. Review each version of the terminology extraction list.

7. Repeat *Step 6* until you find the terminology extraction list that fits your project best.

🗣 For instructions on how to export your
terminology extraction list, see the section
EXPORTING TERMS on page 45.

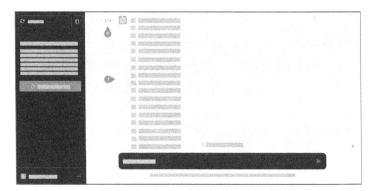

Create a monolingual glossary with ChatGPT

🗣 Creating a monolingual glossary can help you
translate faster and deliver better quality. With just
one prompt, you can create a monolingual glossary
that includes the most important information about
a term: part of speech, gender (in certain languages),
example sentence, and, best of all, a definition. But for
unfamiliar terms or when ChatGPT misinterprets the
context, ChatGPT may provide incorrect definitions.
That means that using ChatGPT to define unknown
terms is not a substitute for doing term research.

1. Open your source document in a suitable program.
   Select and copy the text from which you want to
   extract terms.

2. On the web page **ChatGPT**, in the field **Send a message**: enter one of the following prompts:

🗣 Click the button **Clear chat** near the top of the web page before you enter a prompt. This step clears the chat history, which means that your prompt is not influenced by previous conversations. If you have chat history enabled: click the button **New chat.**

```
Create a table of the terminology
that is used in the following text.
In the table, provide the following
information: term, part of speech,
example sentence, definition.
```

```
Create a table of the words and
expressions in the following text
that may be difficult to translate.
In the table, provide the following
information: term, part of speech,
sentence from the text.
```

🗣 Try out different variations of these prompts and then select the one that fits your project best.

You can use other data categories in your prompt. Use only data categories you need for your project. The more data categories you use, the longer it takes to complete the table.

It's possible to include the data category 'word frequency' in your prompt. But numeric calculations are a known weakness of ChatGPT. Values for word frequency that ChatGPT calculates are unreliable and often wrong.

3. After the prompt that you just entered: paste the text that you copied in *Step 1* into the field **Send a message.**

4. Click the **arrow symbol** > in the field **Send a message.**

   → ChatGPT creates a glossary for the text that you entered.

5. Once ChatGPT has created a glossary: click the button **Regenerate**.

   → ChatGPT creates another glossary for the text that you entered.

🗣 *Steps 5-7* are optional. Use this option if you want to create multiple glossaries and then select the one that fits your project best.

6. Once you have created several versions of the glossary: click the < > arrows at the top of the glossary to navigate between the different versions. Review each version of the glossary.

7. Repeat *Step 6* until you find the glossary that fits your project best.

8. Once you have selected a glossary: click the button **Continue generating** at the bottom of the glossary.

    → ChatGPT continues creating your glossary.

    🗣 If you are using only a few data categories, the button **Continue generating** may not be displayed.

9. Repeat *Step 8* until the glossary is complete.

For instructions on how to export your glossary, see the section EXPORTING TERMS on page 45.

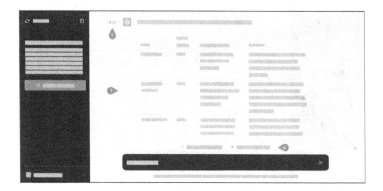

Create a multilingual glossary with ChatGPT

🎙 Creating a multilingual glossary is one of the most powerful features that ChatGPT offers in terms of automatic terminology extraction. With this feature, you can quickly create a draft of a multilingual glossary with definitions and translated terms. Previously, this task could take hours or even days. But for terms that ChatGPT is not familiar with, the chatbot may translate these terms literally and incorrectly. That means that using ChatGPT to translate unknown terms is not a substitute for doing term research. Using ChatGPT to translate terms can still be valuable: when ChatGPT does translate terms correctly, it

saves you time because you don't have to enter those
terms manually.

1. Open your source document in a suitable program.
   Select and copy the text from which you want to
   extract terms.

2. On the web page **ChatGPT**, in the field **Send a
   message:** enter one of the following prompts:

   🗣 Click the button **Clear chat** near the top of the
   web page before you enter a prompt. When you do
   that, you clear the chat history and your prompt
   is not influenced by previous conversations.
   If you have chat history enabled: click the
   button **New chat.**

```
Create a table of the terminology
that is used in the following text.
In the table, provide the following
information: term, translation
in [language].
```

```
Create a table of the words and
expressions in the following text
that may be difficult to translate.
In the table, provide the following
information: term, translation
in [language].
```

For the placeholder [language], enter the name of the target
language. After "translation in [language]", add one or

more additional data categories (examples: part of speech, gender, example sentence from the source text, definition) that fit your project best.

- 🗣 Try out different variations of these prompts to get the best result.

  You can use other data categories in your prompt. Use only data categories you need for your project. The more data categories you specify, the longer it takes to complete the table.

  It's possible to include the data category word frequency in your prompt. But numeric calculations are a known weakness of ChatGPT. Values for word frequency that ChatGPT calculates are unreliable and often wrong.

3. After the prompt that you just entered: paste the text that you copied in *Step 1* into the field **Send a message.**

4. Click the **arrow symbol** > in the field **Send a message.**

   → ChatGPT crea tes a glossary for the text that you entered.

5. Once ChatGPT has created a glossary: click the button **Regenerate**.

    → ChatGPT creates another glossary for the text that you entered.

    🗩 *Steps 5-7* are optional. Use this option to create multiple glossaries and then select the one that fits your project best.

6. Once you have created several versions of the glossary: click the < > arrows at the top of the glossary to navigate between the different versions. Review each version of the glossary.

7. Repeat *Step 6* until you find the glossary that fits your project best.

8. Once you have selected a glossary: click the button **Continue generating** at the bottom of the terminology extraction list.

    → ChatGPT continues creating your terminology extraction list.

- If you are using only a few data categories, the button **Continue generating** may not be displayed.

9. Repeat *Step 8* until the glossary is complete.

- For instructions on how to export your glossary, see the section EXPORTING TERMS on page 45.

Exporting terms

Copy and paste individual terms

🔊 Exporting individual terms with copy and paste is a simple process. Since you can paste text directly into other programs, there's no need for data conversion. When you want to export 30 terms or more, copying and pasting individual terms is not efficient. For those kinds of projects, download the entire glossary.

1. On the web page **ChatGPT**, once your glossary is complete: select and copy the term or other text that you want to export.

2. Paste the term or other text that you want to export into a program of your choice (examples: translation memory program, terminology management program, spreadsheet program).

3. Repeat *Steps 1-2* until you have processed all terms that you want to copy.

→ The glossary is now available for additional processing in the program of your choice.

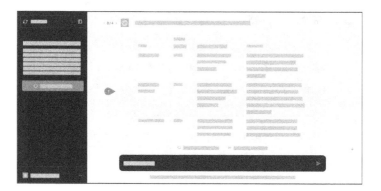

Download the entire glossary

🗣 Downloading is the fastest and most efficient way to export glossaries with 30 terms or more. Downloading is more complex than copying and pasting data as you must complete data conversion during the import process. When you want to export only a few terms, or use the simplest process possible, copy and paste individual terms.

1. On the web page **ChatGPT**, once your glossary is complete: click the **copy symbol** next to your glossary.

2. Paste the glossary into a table or spreadsheet in a program of your choice (examples: terminology management program, translation memory program, or spreadsheet program).

→ The glossary is now available for additional processing in the program of your choice.

How to use OneClick Terms to extract terminology

Finding terms in anonymous mode

Open your source document

1. In your web browser, in the address bar: enter the following web address:
    https://terms.sketchengine.eu/select

    → The web page **Extract Terminology From** opens.

    🗣 In anonymous mode, you won't be able to see or download all terms. But you are able to try out OneClick Terms without logging in or creating an account in Sketch Engine.

2. On the web page **Extract Terminology From:** click the button **One language.**

→ The web page **OneClick Terms Upload** opens.

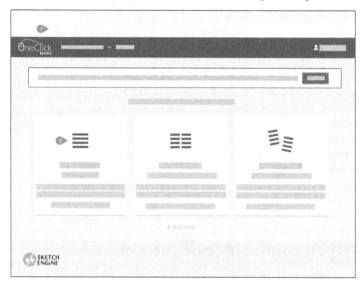

3. On the web page **OneClick Terms Upload**, in the menu **Select language of documents**: click the language of your source document.

4. Click the button **Confirm**.

5. In the field **Upload your files:** click the button **Choose one or more files**.

→ The window **Open** opens.

6. In the window **Open**: navigate to your source document and select your source document.

    🗣 You can select more than one source document. All source documents must be in the same language.

7. Click the button **Open**.

    → The window **Open** closes.

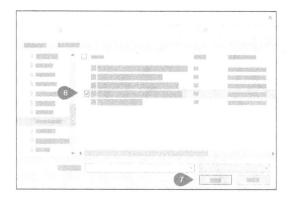

Create a complex terminology extraction list with Sketch Engine

1. On the web page **OneClick Terms Upload:** click the button **More settings**.

→ The window **Settings** opens.

2. In the window **Settings**, under **Give Preference**
    to: move the slider all the way to the right towards
    common words.

    🗣 With this setting, you will find the most terms and
    expressions. If you only want to extract unusual
    terms: use the default setting.

3. Click the button **Save & Close.**

   → The window **Settings** closes.

4. On the web page **OneClick Terms Upload:** click the button **Extract terminology.**

➔ The web page **Your Results** opens.

Exporting terms

Copy and paste individual terms

🗣 Exporting individual terms with copy and paste is a simple process. Since you can paste text directly into other programs, there's no need for data conversion. Also, in OneClick Terms, when you copy and paste, you can manually add terms that the program has missed. When you want to export 30 terms or more, copying and pasting individual terms is not efficient. For those kinds of projects, download the entire glossary.

1. On the web page **YOUR RESULTS**, on the tab **SINGLE-WORDS**: click the check box Show statistics.

   → Word frequency data are displayed as well as other data.

   🗣 This step is optional. Use this option if you want to use word frequency data to select terms for your glossary.

2. In the column **Term**, when you find a term that you want to copy: click the square symbol next to the term.

   → The web page **Examples** opens.

3. On the web page **Examples**: select and copy the term and paste that term into a program of your choice (examples: translation memory program, terminology management program, spreadsheet program). Then, select and copy any expression you want to export and paste that expression into the program of your choice.

4. Close the web page **Examples**.

→ The web page **YOUR RESULTS** opens.

5. On the tab **SINGLE-WORDS:** repeat Steps 2-4 until you have copied and pasted all new terms into the program of your choice.

6. On the web page **YOUR RESULTS:** click the tab **MULTI-WORDS.**

→ Expressions are displayed as well as additional data.

7. In the column **Term**, when you find a term that you want to copy: click the square symbol next to the term.

   → The web page **Examples** opens.

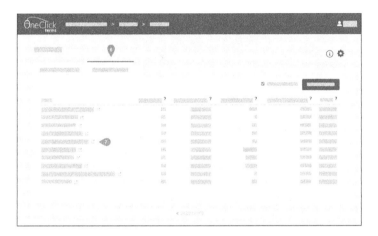

8. On the web page **Examples**: select and copy the term and paste that term into a program of your choice (examples: translation memory program, terminology management program, spreadsheet program). Then, select and copy any expression you want to export and paste that expression into the program of your choice.

9. Close the web page **Examples**.

   → The web page **YOUR RESULTS** opens.

10. On the tab **MULTI-WORDS:** repeat *Steps 2-4* until you have copied and pasted all new terms into the program of your choice.

    → The glossary is now available for additional processing in the program of your choice.

Download the entire glossary (only available with a paid subscription)

🗣 Downloading is the fastest and most efficient way to export glossaries with 30 terms or more. Downloading is more complex than copying and pasting individual terms as you must complete data conversion during the import process. For projects where it's important to create the most complete glossary, downloading the entire glossary in OneClick Term is not ideal. For those kinds of projects, copy and paste individual terms.

1. On the web page **YOUR RESULTS:** click the tab **SINGLE-WORDS.**

2. Click the button **DOWNLOAD**....

    → The window **DOWNLOAD** opens.

3. In the window **DOWNLOAD**, in the field **Number of lines to download**: enter a number that's suitable for your project.

    ✊ This step is optional. Use this option if:

    •   You only want to download a few terms.

    •   There are more than 100 terms in the terminology extraction list, and you want to download all of the terms.

4. Click the check box **Export with examples.**

    🎤 This step is optional. Use this option if you want to use example sentences in your glossary.

5. In the field **Number of examples per line:** enter a number that's suitable for your project.

    🎤 This step is optional. Use this option if you want to have multiple sentences to choose from when you select an example sentence.

6. Click the button **Download.**

    → Your terminology extraction list is downloaded to the folder **Downloads** on your computer.

7. On the web page **YOUR RESULTS:** click the tab **MULTI-WORDS.**

8. Click the button **DOWNLOAD**....

 → The window **DOWNLOAD** opens.

9. In the window **DOWNLOAD**, in the field **Number of lines to download:** enter a number that's suitable for your project.

   🎙 This step is optional. If any of the following statements apply to your project, then changing the number of lines to download might be a good choice for you:

   • You want to download only a small number of terms.

   • You want to make sure that you download all terms if there are more than 100 terms in the terminology extraction list.

10. Click the check box **Export with examples.**

🗣 This step is optional. Use this option if you want to use example sentences in your glossary.

11. In the field **Number of examples per line:** enter a number that's suitable for your project.

🗣 This step is optional. Use this option if you want to have multiple sentences to choose from when you select an example sentence.

12. Click the button **Download**.

→ Your terminology extraction list is downloaded to the folder **Downloads** on your computer.

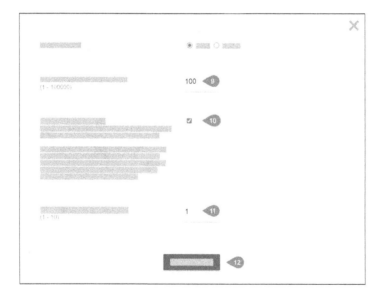

How to use Wordlist Tool to extract terminology

Finding terms

Create a simple terminology extraction list with Wordlist Tool

1. In your web browser, in the address bar: enter the following web address:
    https://www.webcorp.org.uk/live/wdlist.jsp

    → The web page **Generate Wordlist** opens.

2. To read the terms of use: click the link **Terms and conditions.**

    🗣 This step is optional. Use this option to get information about possible risks when you use Wordlist Tool.

3. Under the field **URL**: click the link **Or specify the text to analyse.**

    → A new web page **Generate Wordlist** opens.

🗣 If your source document is available online: enter the web address in the field **URL** and then continue with *Step 5*.

4. Open your source document in a suitable program. Select and copy the text from which you want to create a terminology extraction list.

5. In your web browser, on the web page **Generate Wordlist,** under the field **Copy and paste the text to analyze here:** paste the text that you copied in *Step 3.*

6. In the menu **Minimum Frequency:** change the number for word frequency to **1**.

🗣 It's important that you change the number for word frequency to 1. When you do that, you can make sure that you find all terms.

7. Click the button **Remove URLs.**

🗣 This step is optional. Use this option if you aren't sure that your source document doesn't include any web addresses.

If you entered a web address in *Step 2*, this option is not available.

8. Click the button **Submit**.

→ The web page **Wordlist** opens.

Exporting terms

Copy and paste individual terms

🗣 Exporting individual terms with copy and paste is a simple process. Since you can paste text directly into other programs, there's no need for data conversion. Also, in Wordlist Tool, when you copy and paste, you can manually add terms and expressions that the program has missed. When you want to export 30 terms or more, copying and pasting individual terms is not efficient. For those kinds of projects, download the entire glossary.

1. On the web page **Wordlist**, in the column **Word**, when you find a term that you want to copy: click the term.

→ The web page **Single Document Search** opens.

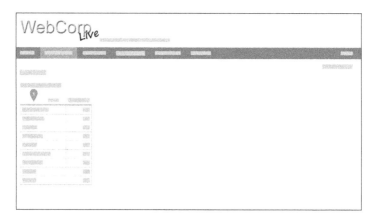

2. On the web page **Single Document Search:** select and copy the term and paste that term into a program of your choice (examples: translation memory program, terminology management program, spreadsheet program). Then, select and copy any related expression, and paste that expression into the program of your choice.

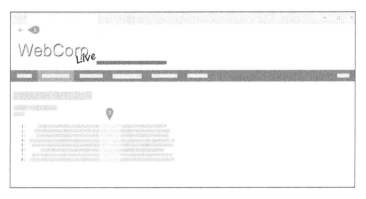

3. Click the **back button**.

   → The web page **Wordlist** opens.

4. Repeat *Steps 1-3* until you have processed all terms that you want to copy.

   → The glossary is now available for additional processing in the program of your choice.

Download the entire glossary

🎙️ Downloading is the fastest and most efficient way to export glossaries with 30 terms or more. Downloading is more complex than copying and pasting individual terms as you must complete data conversion during the import process. For projects where it's important to create the most complete glossary, downloading the entire glossary in Wordlist Tool is not ideal. For those kinds of projects, copy and paste individual terms.

1. On the web page **Wordlist**: select and copy the terms that you want to export.

2. Paste the glossary into a table or spreadsheet in a program of your choice (examples: terminology management program, translation memory program, or spreadsheet program).

   → The glossary is now available for additional processing in the program of your choice.

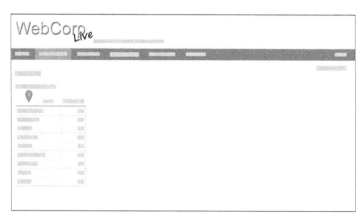

Glossary

The following definitions explain how I use certain terms in this book.

a

account   an identity that you create to be able to use a computer or a program

address bar   a field in a web browser that displays the web address of a web page

anonymous mode   a mode where you can use a program for free, with some functions unavailable, without creating an account

b

back button   an element in the graphical user interface of a web browser that lets you navigate to the previous web page

button   an element in a graphical user interface that you can click to select an object or to control a program

c

captcha   a program that's designed to allow access to a website to people and deny access to other programs

character   a symbol that people use in written communication

chat   a conversation between you and a chatbot

chatbot   a program that's based on artificial intelligence and that simulates human conversation with you through text

check box   an element in a graphical user interface
                       where you can select one or more options

click   to push and release a push-button on
                       an input device to select an object in a
                       graphical user interface

client   a person or organization that pays you to
                       work on a translation project

computer   an electronic device that uses programs to
                       perform specific tasks

computer network   a group of computers that are connected
                       so that they can communicate with each
                       other

confidential   relating to information that should to be
                       kept secret

content   anything that represents meaningful
                       information or knowledge

context   the words that come immediately before
                       and after a specific word or expression
                       that help explain the meaning of that
                       specific word or expression

copy   to duplicate selected data so that you can
                       move that data to a different location

copy and paste   the process of duplicating selected data
                       and moving that data to a different
                       location

customize   to change something so that it fits a
                       particular requirement or a personal
                       preference

d

data
information that can be stored electronically on a computer

data category
the linguistic properties that can be used to organize the information that goes into glossary entries (examples: part of speech, gender, example sentence)

data conversion
the process of transforming information from one format or structure to another

default setting
a setting that a program uses automatically

delivery time
the time within which a translation project is completed and submitted to the client

device
any electronic equipment that can run programs

document
an electronic file that contains text and possibly other types of data

download
to transfer data from the internet or another computer to your own device

e

efficient
relating to doing things in a smart and organized way to save time and energy

email
an electronic message that you send from one computer to one or more other computers via a computer network

email address
a digital address that you use to send and receive emails

email system
a program for sending and receiving emails

estimate
a rough calculation of the cost and time required to complete a project

expression	a group of two or more words that express a thought but that don't form a complete sentence
extract	to identify and collect important words from a source document
f	
field	an area in a graphical user interface where you can enter data
folder	a storage location for documents on a computer
font	a set of typographic elements for displaying text in a certain style
frequency-based	relating to a method that analyzes the number of times a word appears in a text
g	
gender	a data category that assigns certain types of words to two or more classes in some languages
glossary	a document that contains the terms and their definitions that are used in a project or a field of knowledge
graphical user interface	a user interface that allows you to control a program through graphical elements such as symbols, buttons, and windows
h	
hardware	the physical components of a computer
i	
input device	a device that allows you to interact with your computer
intellectual property	the creations of the human mind that an individual or organization owns and that the law protects from unauthorized use by others

interact　　　　　　　　to act upon or have an effect on something

internet　　　　　　　　a global computer network that's open to the public

internet connection　　the link that allows you to access and use the internet on your device

interpretation　　　　　the process of creating content in a target language from content in a source language in spoken form

intuitive　　　　　　　　relating to the ability to understand something without getting instructions

j

joy of work　　　　　　a feeling of happiness that you get when a project goes well

junk folder　　　　　　a storage location for emails that you or your email system identify as unwanted

l

language　　　　　　　a system of communication in written or spoken form

language specialist　　a person who provides services like interpretation, translation, or terminology management

large language model　a program that uses large amounts of training data to understand and create human language

linguistic　　　　　　　relating to a method that analyzes a text based on an understanding of the structure of a language

link　　　　　　　　　　a reference, either a text or an image, that takes you to a different location when you click that reference

m

machine translation	the process of creating content in a target language from content in a source language in written form through a translation program, without the help of a language specialist
machine translation program	a program that creates content in a target language from content in a source language in written form without the help of a language specialist
menu	an element in a graphical user interface that gives you a list of options from which you can select
messages app	a program that lets you send and receive text messages on a smartphone
monolingual	relating to content that's available in one language
multilingual	relating to content that's available in more than one language
multi-part term	a term that consists of more than one word

n

name	one or more words that identify a specific person, place, or thing
navigate	to move from one location to another within or between websites or programs

o

operating system	a program that controls how the hardware of your device communicates with other programs
opt out	to withdraw voluntarily from a service

option one element among several elements in a graphical user interface that let you make a choice

optional relating to a situation where you can make a choice

organization a group of people who are working together to achieve a specific result

p

part of speech the data category that identifies the grammatical function of a word

password a secret combination of characters that you use to access a device, program, or account

paste to move selected text from the device memory to a document

peak times the periods of the day when there is a significant increase in activity or demand for a particular service

placeholder text that represents information that you can add

privacy policy a document that describes how an organization collects, uses, shares, and protects personal data

process a set of tasks that you complete as part of a project

product something that you can buy and that can be touched

program a set of instructions that are written so that a device can complete a task

project an effort that one or more persons carry out to achieve a specific result within a specific time period

project-specific   relating to a particular project

prompt   a question that you write to get information from a chatbot

q

quality   the degree to which a product or service meets client expectations

quality assurance   the processes with which you make sure that a product or service meets client expectations

quotation   a document that lists the price and delivery time of a product or service that's being offered

r

revision   the process of reviewing and changing a text to improve its quality, clarity, or correctness

risk   the probability that a project has a negative outcome

s

select   to choose content or activate an element in a graphical user interface

sentence   a group of words that expresses a thought

server   a computer that stores, processes, and distributes data in a computer network

service   something that you can buy but that's not a product

single-part terms   a term that consists of only one word

slider   an element in a graphical user interface that you can move to change a setting in a program

smartphone   a device that combines the functions of a computer and a phone

source document	the original text that you use to complete tasks like translation or terminology extraction
source language	the language that you translate from
special character	a symbol that is different from standard characters and numbers
spreadsheet	a document that contains data that's organized in rows and columns
spreadsheet program	a program that makes it easy to display and analyze data that's organized in rows and columns
step	an action that you complete as part of a task
subscription	an agreement where you pay a fee to use a product or service for a certain period of time
symbol	a sign that represents an object or an idea

t

tab	an element in a graphical user interface that lets you select a sub-menu in a program or on a web page
table	a structure in which data is organized in rows and columns
tablet	a small portable computer with a touchscreen that you can operate with your fingers
target language	the language you translate from
task	a set of steps that you complete as part of a process
term	an important word
term research	the process of finding translated terms for terms in the source language

terms of use	a set of rules that you must agree to follow when you use a program or service
terminological consistency	the state where one term in the source language corresponds to one and only one translated term in a translation project
terminology	the important words in a field of knowledge
terminology extraction	the process of collecting terms
terminology extraction list	a document that contains a collection of terms
terminology management	the process of systematically identifying, organizing, and distributing terminology
terminology management program	a program that makes it easier to complete the tasks that relate to terminology management
text	any content in written form
text analysis program	a program that helps you identify patterns in large texts
text message	a brief electronic message with written text that you can send and receive on your smartphone
toggle	an element in a graphical user interface that you can click to switch a function on or off
trademark	a type of intellectual property that represents an individual, an organization, or a product
translate	to create a document in a target language from a document in a source language
translated term	a word or phrase in a target language that was translated from a term in a source language

translation
the process of creating content in a target language from content in a source language in written form

translation memory program
a program that makes it easier to complete tasks that relate to translation

translation project
a type of project where a language specialist or machine translation program creates content in a target language from content in a source language in written form

turn
one round of conversation between you and a chatbot

u

unknown term
a term in the source language for which you don't know the translated term

upload
to transfer data from your own device to the internet or another computer

user interface
the part of a program that allows you to control that program

w

web address
text that stands for the location of a web page or a web server on the internet

web browser
a program that makes it easier to access information on the internet

web page
a document that's accessible on the internet

web-based
relating to programs that you can access on the internet through a web browser

web-based program
a program that processes data on a server that you can access on the internet through a web browser

website
a collection of web pages on the internet

window a rectangular element of a graphical user interface that displays content or lets you interact with a program

word the smallest unit of meaning in a text (this definition applies only to languages that use words)

word count the number of words in a document

word frequency how often a word appears in a text

www.ingramcontent.com/pod-product-compliance
Lightning Source LLC
LaVergne TN
LVHW051539050326
832903LV00033B/4331